Church Chuckles

Amusing Anecdotes

from

The Life

of

A Church Minister

The Revd. John Carrier

Illustrated by Geoff Southgate

Church Chuckles

Published by Noel Barratt 2011
Copyright© John Carrier 2011

All rights reserved. No part of this publication may be reproduced, stored in a retrieval system or transmitted by any means, without the prior permission of the author

Printed by:
TWP Printing & Copying Ltd.
Royal Leamington Spa
Warwickshire
01926 883757

ISBN 978-0-9567225-1-5

Introduction

I was ordained into the Congregational (later to become the United Reformed) Church Ministry over 50 years ago after a five year training at Lancashire Independent College in Manchester.

It has been a real privilege, as a church minister, to share the joys and sorrows of life with so many people.

I have had opportunities of sharing the happiness of families on the birth of a child and have been present to help other families in their grief at the loss of a relative. I have experienced moments of great joy when two young people are joined in marriage, or the simple sharing of a home as pastoral visits have been undertaken. Sometimes, in all these moments, things don't quite go as planned and something happens, or something is said, which causes a chuckle. This book recalls those moments and every anecdote recounted in these pages is absolutely true.

Those moments made me smile, and I hope that as I share them with you as you read this book, they will bring a smile to your face.

Enjoy,

John

Acknowledgements

WITH GRATEFUL THANKS:

To my wife, Marjorie, whose help, encouragement and practical support in the preparation of the text, has been invaluable.

To my friend, Geoff Southgate, for the illustrations which enhance the text in a unique way.

To my elder daughter, Heather, for patiently proof-reading every word on every page of this book.

To my publisher, Noel Barratt, for all his support and advice.

To Terry Arnold and the staff at TWP Printers for their help in the production of this book.

And to the many people who, on hearing one or two anecdotes, encouraged me to share these true stories with a wider audience.

CONTENTS PAGE

1953	1
In the Beginning	2
College Days	3
College Tour	8
Other Colleges	11
Monthly Bible Exam	14
Sermon Class	18
Sunday Preaching	20
Student Pastorate	26
Organists	32
Building a New Church	35
Sermons	41
Family Services	43
Baptisms	48
Weddings	53
Funerals	58
Visiting	64
Church Notice Boards	66
Special Services	68
Chaplaincy	70
Apocrypha	73

What a year!

1953

1953 was a great year.

Eisenhower won the presidential race by a landslide, defeating Democrat Adlai Stevenson and ending two decades of the New Deal Coalition holding the White House.

It was the year of the East coast floods when, in total, 307 people died, 24,500 houses were damaged and over 30,000 people were evacuated.

It was also the year of Queen Elizabeth II's Coronation and was the first ceremony of this kind in this country to be televised.

It was the year when Hilary and Tensing became the first men to conquer Mount Everest.

It was also the year when the first colour television sets were sold.

Now if that wasn't enough, 1953 was the year when I entered theological college to train for the ministry and that is where I want to begin my anecdotes.

In The Beginning

I left school at the age of fifteen and was delighted to be offered an engineering apprenticeship at Garrard's Engineering Works in Swindon. My father had worked there all his life and so I was following in his footsteps.

As an apprentice my pay was poor and for five years I went back and forth to Garrard's learning more practical skills each day until, finally, I was awarded my Indentures and I was a fully-fledged precision engineer helping to make the tools for the production of clocks, record players and ticket machines.

I had always attended church with my family. I had been a member of the Youth Club and had taken a full role in the life of the church. In my late teens I became a lay preacher and, increasingly, felt that God was calling me to serve Him in a more meaningful way. I decided to candidate for the Congregational Church Ministry and after several rather gruelling interviews by my local church, by the District and by the Province, I was given approval to apply for a place at a theological college.

My mentor, the Minister of my local church, had attended Lancashire Independent College in Manchester many years previously and he felt that I should go there too. I filled in the application form for the five year course and waited. Finally I was called for interview and offered a place at the college.

College Days

Lancashire Independent College, Manchester

Lancashire Independent College was opened in 1843 and constructed with an imposing frontage of Gothic design of the late 15th century period. Huge wrought iron gates opened onto a drive leading to the college's massive oak door. It was an awe-inspiring place with long corridors, high ceilings and a general smell of mustiness and age. On my first day I was shown to my bedroom and, after a quick inspection of the sparse furnishings – a bed, a wardrobe and a chair, I was allocated my study on the floor below. Here I saw a desk, a wooden upright chair and an open fire. That was it! Those who wanted the luxury of an easy chair had to supply it themselves. This necessitated a visit to a second hand furniture shop in the rather run-down part of Manchester known as Moss Side and then haggling with the shopkeeper to buy the chair as cheaply as possible. The next difficulty was transporting the chair back to college as none of the students, in those days, owned cars. Another student was bribed for the task with the promise of a reciprocal favour when it was needed.

On the first evening at college we assembled in the Great Hall to meet the other students, to have the college routine explained and to get our timetables. At that meeting each of the 'freshers' was allocated a job which they had to undertake during their first year, for the benefit of the college community. My job had the wonderful title 'Master of the Rolls'. This wasn't the marking of a register to ensure that students attended lectures but it entailed the regular checking of all the loos to ensure that they were well stocked with the necessary rolls of paper.

Dinner was a formal meal when all staff and students assembled together. Protocol dictated that all the new students sat together at one end of the dining room furthest from the top table where the Principal and senior staff were seated. As the years passed, you moved up the dining room until in the final year you would be sharing a table with the staff. Ten students were seated at each table – four on each side and one at each end. At the head of each table a senior student would preside and he would be responsible for serving the food. The meals were certainly not cordon bleu but we were all young, healthy and hungry and so we ate with relish.

This wasn't in the job description!

Students were of varying ages and had had a range of occupations before coming to college. Much of the humour learned in previous work became evident in the early days of college life. There was a lot of discussion about their earlier employment prior to becoming college students. Amongst the students in my year there was a commercial traveller, a theatre manager, a secretary, a wages' clerk and a carpenter. I had been an engineer.

We socialised a lot together and one day when we were drinking tea (part of theological training!), we discovered that one of the students had come straight from school.
Everyone was aghast.
"You can't say that, you must invent a job," we chided. He would be teased unmercifully if this fact were known.
We persuaded him that if anyone asked what his earlier work had been he was to say that he had been a hairdresser. We knew that it was more than likely that, before too long, he would be asked by a fellow student if he would cut his hair. We planned to procure the necessary equipment so that he looked like a professional barber. He was happy to go along with this plan as he did not want to appear naïve in the eyes of his peers.

As is the case today, students are always short of money and when word spread that there was an ex-barber in our midst someone suggested that this new student should cut students' hair at a very reasonable rate. It didn't take many days before someone approached him and asked for a short back and sides. The customer was seated in the chair and a towel was draped around his shoulders. The 'barber', armed with scissors and clippers, started to cut the hair of the unsuspecting victim. The pseudo-barber didn't have a clue what to do and within a few minutes there was hair all over the floor and suddenly the top of his victim's head was practically bald!

He looked such a mess that when the Principal heard about it and saw the resulting 'hair cut' he had no alternative but to exempt the unfortunate student from any preaching engagements for the next three weeks until his hair had grown to a respectable length!

Please God, make it grow!

College Tour

The front of Northern College was a very imposing stone building and gave the impression of being a stately home rather than a theological college. However, the rear of the building was entirely different and instead of the fine stonework one saw at the front there were just ordinary plain brick walls. It has often been described as having a Queen Anne front and a Mary Ann back.

The entrance to the front of the college was through a pair of large, decorative wrought iron gates beyond which there was a wide gravel path, flanked on both side with immaculate lawns of which our gardener was justly proud. The gravel path led to the steps which took the visitor up to the solid wooden front door.

Strangely, there was no notice by the gates to indicate that the building was a college for theological students. On one occasion a student was just leaving by the main entrance when he was stopped by a passer-by who engaged him in conversation and enquired what the building was.
The student thought quickly and, without as much as a glint in his eye, replied,
"Oh it's an asylum for religious maniacs."
"Well," replied the stranger, "I didn't know there were such places."

The gates of Lancashire Independent College

The student was obviously enjoying this pretence and elaborated on the mental state of the inmates at this 'institution'. He got so carried away by the elaborate picture he was painting in the stranger's mind that he offered to show his astounded listener around the building. He said that, unfortunately, he could not do it there and then, but if the stranger returned in two days time at 3 o'clock he would be happy to give him a conducted tour. The stranger was delighted with this offer and put the appointment in his diary.

During the following two days the student body was alerted about the impending visit of a stranger who had been led to believe that the college was an asylum for religious maniacs and all agreed to act accordingly when the visitor arrived.

At the appointed time the visitor was met by the student and taken into the building. He was utterly amazed by what he saw. There were students sitting in corners with open Bibles and others waving Bibles at the visitor. The guide took the unsuspecting visitor into the library and explained that all the books were of a religious theme as the 'inmates' refused to read anything but religious books! The pretence went on as the visitor was shown various rooms including individual studies, the dining room and the chapel. Throughout his visit every student entered into the spirit of the prank and quoted Greek or Hebrew passages as he passed by.

After the tour the student escorted the open-mouthed visitor to the gates and the parting comment from him was,
"Can I book a group to come back next week?"

Other Colleges

There was always great rivalry between Lancashire College and the neighbouring Hartley Victoria Methodist College. The proximity of these two theological colleges and the fact that one was for training Congregational Ministers whilst the other was for the training of Methodist Ministers caused nearly as much friction as that experienced by Oxford and Cambridge colleges in the boat race. This intense competition between the two colleges reached its climax when the football teams of the two colleges met in the inter-college football league. It did not matter if we lost every other football match in the season as long as we beat the Methodists. We tolerated defeat by the Baptist College but we treated the Methodists as our arch-enemies and we would go to any lengths, fair or foul, to beat them. They were vicious encounters with no holds barred (as long as the referee wasn't looking), and I still have scars on my legs from those matches. It was customary that whichever team proved victorious would perpetrate an after-match jape on their rivals.

On one occasion, following a win by Lancashire College, some of the victors secretly entered the Methodist College whilst all the students were in a meeting. The dining room was located and all the cutlery was stolen. Having achieved their aim they retreated with the booty and issued a ransom for its return. This was to be a donation to Lancashire College's Mission Fund.

It was supposed to be a friendly match!

On another occasion, (following yet another win by Lancashire College), the joke back-fired on the victorious team. The Lancashire College team placed a spoof advertisement in The Manchester Evening Newspaper stating that a jumble sale was to be held at Hartley College and that all jumble should be left on the main steps of the Methodist College on a specified day. The perpetrators imagined a whole mountain of unwanted clothing and other junk amassing there and causing mayhem. Sure enough, on the appointed day the sacks of unwanted clothing and other garbage accumulated on the college steps. The pile got bigger and bigger as the locals responded to the request for unwanted jumble for the sale.

This caused great amusement at the time but later they had the last laugh. The Methodist students decided that they would, in fact, hold a jumble sale to sell all the unwanted and unsolicited 'rubbish'. This they did, and much to our chagrin, raised a considerable sum of money.

Monthly Bible Exams

College life proceeded in a regular pattern of lectures, seeing girlfriends, reading, going to the pictures, discussion groups, football matches, tutorials with lecturers, having boys' nights out, essays to be written and submitted etc. etc. Often it was a juggling act with the work load vying with social commitments and, more often than not, the social side winning.

However, everyone did settle down to work especially as the monthly Bible Exam loomed nearer and nearer. As theological students we were expected to know the Bible inside out and to have in-depth knowledge of each book. To ensure that each student was studying and learning to the required standard it was deemed essential that regular examinations should take place. These hour long exams were held on the first Saturday morning in every month and each exam focussed on a particular book of the Bible.

As we made a detailed study of each book of the Bible all sorts of interesting facts were revealed. Some of the facts were not those that the early writers had intended. From the Book of Genesis we learned that a popular game of the time was tennis. We discovered this fact because it says, 'Joseph served in the courts of Pharaoh'.

Having made that discovery we vied with each other to find other sports within the Scriptures.

Joseph served in the courts of Pharaoh

In The Acts of the Apostles we found a reference to the game of rugby:
'Paul passed on to Troas.'
Golf was mentioned in the Bible too because we read the following: 'and his driving was like the driving of Jehu' (2 Kings 9 v. 20).
For those who were card sharps there was a strict warning, 'Wist ye not' (Luke 2:v. 49).

One of the college professors tried to make the examination interesting with questions phrased in an unusual way. For example, when we were studying the book of Jeremiah we were asked,
'Was Jeremiah a bachelor?'
One student's answer was very brief and was written in a matter of seconds.
He answered,
'No. Jeremiah was not a bachelor because he cursed the day that he was born.' (Jer. 20: v.14).
It wasn't quite the answer the professor had anticipated!

In the course of our studies we also discovered that Bildad was the smallest man in the Bible. We read in Job 42 v. 9 that Bilbad was a Shuhite (shoe height) and the second smallest man was Nehemiah (knee high Miah).

We also discovered that Moses may have suffered from constipation because he took two tablets and went into a mountain.

In 1953 most theological students were men. This was in the days when girls usually trained to be nurses, secretaries or teachers and generally speaking it was men who sought to be train drivers, engineers and church ministers. There was only one female student in college in my day. She was not allowed to live in the male dominated confines of the college but had a room at the YWCA hostel across the road. She attended college for lectures and meals. One day she arrived at college and promptly stated that she had Biblical evidence that men should always make the tea. On being asked for an explanation for this statement she opened the New Testament and pointed to the top of several pages which said 'Hebrews'.

Sermon Class

There are excellent sermons which stimulate and inspire the congregation. There are good sermons that make the congregation think a little. There are poor sermons when the church attendees think that they themselves could have preached better sermons and where their minds drift to other things. There are occasionally appalling sermons where the regular churchgoers wish they had had an extra hour in bed. One Minister used to say that if all those who slept during his sermons were laid out end to end……. then they would be a lot more comfortable!

During my five year training we attended Sermon Classes each week to make us aware of the necessity to state our doctrine in clear concise ways and to present our thoughts in a coherent and inspirational manner. Not only had the service to be well planned and thoughtfully presented but there had to be a pre-determined structure to the sermon so that people would benefit from listening. We were also trained in voice projection techniques, in stance and body language and in conducting ourselves in a proper manner.

A Sermon Class was held each week in which each student in turn had to prepare a sermon and preach it in the college chapel to a congregation comprising of staff and fellow students. It was an ordeal to stand up in front of such a critical company. After the

service everyone adjourned to the classroom where a discussion and critique on the content and presentation of the sermon were made. Some of the comments could be quite brutal, but also very witty. One student preached a sermon which was quite poor and a fellow student, trying not to be too harsh, said,
"I think the idea was well conceived."
It was immediately followed by another student's observation "You think it was well conceived do you? It might have been well conceived, but it was painfully laboured and badly delivered."

Christians awake!

Sunday Preaching

Students were invited to lead worship in different churches all over Lancashire, Cheshire and West Yorkshire. This was a very useful way of preparing trainee ministers for the time when they were ordained. No two services were exactly the same and one had to adapt to the individual circumstances. On occasions there was a large congregation, at other times one faced half a dozen elderly ladies who gathered together each week for worship. Sometimes the Church Secretary greeted you with the words, "Mrs-So-and-So died this week, would you say special prayers for the family?" or "Our organist can't make it this morning. Can you lead the singing unaccompanied? One had to adapt to these differing circumstances quickly and efficiently.

In those days no student possessed a car and so it meant undertaking quite lengthy journeys by bus or train to reach outlying destinations. Often students arrived back in Manchester late at night and then had to catch a bus from Piccadilly, in the centre of Manchester, to the College in Whalley Range. One of my friends, having conducted two Sunday services at a church many miles away, arrived back in the centre of Manchester late at night. His connecting bus which would take him on the last lap of his journey back to college was not due to leave for another half hour. He sat on one of the seats in Piccadilly Gardens close to the bus terminus.

Piccadilly had a notorious reputation at that time as it was part of the red light district frequented by 'ladies of the night'.
Whilst my friend was sitting on the seat one of the local prostitutes came and sat down beside him. It was not long before she gave him a nudge and a 'come on' nod of the head. My friend ignored the proposition and so the process was repeated.
Eventually he stood up in front of the lady and, without saying a word, pointed to the dog collar he was wearing. She immediately jumped up and faced him – took hold of the lapels of his overcoat, wrapped them across his chest to cover his dog collar and said,
"Forget that, come on let's have some fun."

Going out preaching was always interesting. This was particularly true when you reached the point in the service where the Church Secretary read out the notices for the coming week. This was in the days before computers were used to put announcements on Powerpoint presentations and project them on a big screen at the front of the church. It was even before the time when weekly news sheets were given out to the members of the congregation as they arrived for the service. It was the Church Secretary's big moment to announce the coming events and all eyes were upon him.

On one occasion, as the details of the forthcoming Church outing were announced, the secretary declared,

"The convenience will leave the church at 10.30am."
I wondered if they were having an outing to Flushing Meadow!

I tried to arrange my Sunday preaching engagements so that I led services at churches in West Yorkshire where Marjorie (to whom I was engaged and who is now my wife), lived. We would arrange to meet and then travel to the church together. On one particular Sunday when this happened I was welcomed to the service and the secretary declared to the congregation that, "John has also brought his financier with him."

After one Church Secretary had extended a welcome to everyone and announced that Scouts would meet on Monday, the Women's Hour on Tuesday, the Youth Group on Wednesday etc. he said, "Next Sunday the preacher will be the Rev. W. Gordon Robinson M.A., B.D., Ph.D."
Everything went well until he reached the Ph.D. Instead of pronouncing the abbreviation in the normal way he used the phonetic pronunciation: F D. There were restrained giggles from some members of the congregation and it was really difficult for me to keep a straight face.

Many of the churches visited by the students did not have a resident incumbent but relied on the college for a regular supply of preachers. Not only did students preach in these churches but the staff and the principal also were on the preaching list. It became quite a bandwagon and the names of the previous Sunday's preacher and that of the preacher for the following Sunday were often recognised by the visiting student. One Sunday I was preaching at a particular church and the preacher on the following Sunday was to be the Principal of the college.

The Principal was an outstanding academic, with a string of letters after his name. He had a very likeable personality. Many other people with such brilliant minds find it difficult to relate to the ordinary man-in-the-street, but he had that enviable ability to converse easily with everyone he met. When it came to planning and preparing Sunday services he did it superbly. He was a renowned preacher and a genius at giving children's addresses and everyone who heard him was spellbound by the stories he told. He could take an ordinary situation and, whilst relating a story or incident during the children's slot in a service, was able to make three points which the children could remember.

One day I was travelling on a bus with him and we were discussing this technique of interesting the listeners and holding their attention whilst emphasising the message behind the story. "It is easy", he declared. "You just take any ordinary situation and think of three ideas connected with what you see". He was about to expand on how he managed this when we reached a bus stop and the bus drew in to allow passengers to dismount. As we looked out of the window there was a girl doing a handstand against the wall. I challenged him to find three points for my next children's address using that situation. He thought for a moment and then said,
"Firstly you need a good sense of balance in life. Secondly, you must look at the world the right way up. And thirdly, if you are going to do handstands make sure you are wearing clean knickers!"

There is an art in preaching and being able to hold the congregation's attention whilst you talk and get your message across to them in a limited time. If your sermon is too brief the congregation feel short-changed; if it's too long some fall asleep whilst others lose the thread of the message and their minds wander. It has been known for members of a congregation to count the organ pipes during a rather boring sermon or to play a mental game of Sudoku using the numbers on the hymn boards! A fifteen minute sermon is considered ideal in the United Reformed Church. One of the things we were told to observe when preparing our sermons was,
"If you can't strike oil in fifteen minutes, stop boring."

I've struck oil - without boring!

Student Pastorate

Although the majority of university and college students enjoy long summer holidays and lengthy breaks at Easter and Christmas things are a little different for students of theology. During each of the summer recesses over the five years of the course, each student was expected to have a student pastorate. This entailed finding a temporary appointment in a church for three months during the long summer vacation. A member of the church would be expected to offer free board and lodgings and the student was able to claim travel and incidental expenses but did not receive any remuneration for his work. It was felt that this 'grass roots' experience would be invaluable in his future ministry.

Each student was expected to set up his own student pastorate and although the college staff would not oversee the work he did in this venture, detailed records of the experiences had to be kept. These would later be examined and discussed so that the student could learn from any mistakes he had made and share the experiences he had encountered with other students when he returned to college. Not only were students expected to preach on Sundays but they visited those in pastoral need, attended mid-week meetings, led youth groups, conducted funerals and generally took on the role as locum Minister. It was usual for students to choose a small church which did not have a full time Minister but which would benefit and appreciate the help a student could give albeit for a limited time.

In my fourth year at college I spent my student pastorate at Belle Isle Church in Leeds. The reason for this choice was that it was within a couple of miles of Marjorie's home and we would be able to see each other in whatever spare time I had. By this time Marjorie and I were engaged and making plans for our wedding the following summer. Belle Isle, although bearing the grand French name meaning Beautiful Isle, was, in fact, a council estate in a suburb of Leeds with a rather dubious reputation. The Church building was a small brick building in the centre of the estate and its dual purpose construction enabled it to be used for both weekday activities and for Sunday worship. At one end of the hall was the sanctuary with communion table, pulpit, lectern and organ. This could be partitioned off with a sliding screen. At the other end of the hall was the stage, with a similar partitioning screen. This meant that the access to the hall was in the centre of one of the long walls. There was a long corridor parallel to the hall with rooms, kitchen and toilets leading off. During my first service in the church, halfway through my sermon and when I felt the congregation was in the palm of my hand, the organist got up, walked across the sanctuary, down the centre aisle and out through the door halfway down the church. This disturbance ruined the atmosphere. Just as I reached the climax of the sermon the door opened and the organist returned down the aisle, across the sanctuary and back to the organ.

On my second Sunday the same thing happened. Halfway through the sermon the organist got to his feet, walked across the sanctuary, down the aisle, out through the door and returned just before the end of the sermon. There was a repeat performance on the third week. These regular weekly interruptions were most

disruptive, both to me and to the congregation and I knew I must do something about it. After the third service was over I went up to him. In the most tactful manner I could muster, I broached the subject and asked if it were really necessary for these regular disturbances. He completely took the wind out of my sails by saying in his blunt Yorkshire accent,
"Vicar, it's me bladder you know."

It was whilst I was at Belle Isle that I had to go and visit a lady in Hunslet. This area of the city was one of the oldest and poorest parts of Leeds. The houses were in terraces, constructed back to back, the front door opened directly onto the street and the privy, shared by several houses, was at the end of the terrace. The houses were known as "one up, one down" as there was just one room upstairs and one room downstairs. Each family lived in very cramped conditions and there was no privacy. I understood what that meant when I called to see this particular lady. She opened the front door and I was invited in. Shock, horror! There, sitting in a galvanised bath placed in front of the fire was the lady's granddaughter, a well endowed teenager who was completely naked. The grandmother thought nothing of inviting me in and the girl was not embarrassed either. It was only me who had a very red face! I quickly learned that ministers have to be un-shockable AND also have not to laugh at incidents which are quite funny.

Was my face red?

People jokingly say to me that Ministers of Religion only work on Sundays but that really isn't the case. There are sermons to write, Bible Study Groups to lead, Uniformed Organisations and Youth Clubs to visit and Elders' Meetings and Finance Committees to chair.

One is constantly asked to speak at Women's Friendship Circles, Darby and Joan Clubs, Gardening Groups, Women's Institutes and even Golf Clubs.

Then there is visiting to do. Pastoral visiting is an important part of Christian ministry and must be carried out sympathetically and in a caring manner. Some people are terribly lonely and do not have a close family, friends or neighbours to pop in to see them. When the minister calls they just want to talk and talk and talk. Others are in need of prayers especially at critical times in their lives whilst others need counselling because of some traumatic event which has affected them deeply. Often Ministers are privy to thoughts and confidences which cannot be divulged to anyone else because people trust that Ministers to keep these confidences.

One day I called to see a lady who I had not seen in church for some time. She explained to me that she was having problems with her feet as she had very bad corns. I asked if she had done anything to alleviate the problem and she told me that she had bought some corn plasters.
"Are they doing any good?" I enquired.

She explained that she had put them on her painful feet but that, at the moment she wasn't wearing them. She said,
"Well, I haven't got them now as I went to the Darby & Joan Club last Friday and I took the plasters off my feet and have lent them to a friend who has the same problem".

On another occasion I visited a lady about eleven o'clock in the morning and hoped that she would invite me to have a cup of coffee with her. I walked up her drive, rang the bell and waited. Eventually the door opened very slightly. Then a voice came from inside,
"Oh, Mr. Carrier, I'm not dressed yet, do come in."

Organists

Nowadays many churches use music groups to lead the singing during church services. This can be anything from a small quartet of singers to a large group of instrumentalists who take up a vast area with their drum kits, electronic guitars, keyboards, violins, cellos, recorders, flutes, clarinets and other instruments. Youngsters love to play in these groups and many churches find that it is a way of attracting younger people to the church.

In the 1960s and 1970s churches relied on a stalwart organist to lead the hymns. If there was no one able to play then a pianist was the next option.

In my experience organists come in all shapes, sizes and musical abilities. One particular organist I had was not one of the best. As Eric Morecambe might have said,
"She played all the notes, but got them in the wrong order."

Her repertoire was very limited, but one of her favourite pieces was 'Little Donkey'. She looked forward to Christmas, because it meant she could play this piece prior to the commencement of each Sunday service. We walked the stony road with the little donkey and his heavy load every Sunday from the beginning of October until Christmas Day!

Little Donkey, little donkey….

It is essential that ministers and organists work as a team. The organists generally like to have the hymns early in the week preceding a Sunday service, so that they can practice beforehand and so that a choir can rehearse the hymns and thus lead the singing at the service. I visited one village church where there was no request for me to send the hymns in advance. When I arrived at the church on the Sunday, I discovered the reason for this. I went to the vestry and was greeted by the organist who slapped a piece of paper on the table and said,
"These are the twelve hymns I can play, which ones do you want in today's service?"

There is a book called 'Companion to Congregational Praise', which gives background information about all the hymns in the hymn book and can be used to give an introduction to the hymn during a service.

I had selected a certain hymn, 'O, for a thousand tongues to sing', and I used the Companion Book to glean some information about it. It stated that although our hymn book showed six verses for the hymn, the original version had eighteen verses! I informed the congregation of this fact and the harmonium, which we were using to supply the musical accompaniment, must have taken great umbrage to this information. No sooner had the organist started to play the introduction to the hymn, than there was a loud bang from the harmonium. The belt on the foot pedal had broken making the instrument unusable and we had to sing the six verses unaccompanied!

A New Church

Today many old churches are closing and the buildings are being converted to some other use. Some are turned into warehouses, others are purchased by an entrepreneur and, with ideas gleaned from the many property conversion programmes which currently dominate television, are transformed into dream homes fit for celebrities.

However, Christianity is not dead and new churches are still being built, many of which attract young families who want to worship God in a modern setting. Styles of service change over the years and whilst some still like the traditions of their forefathers, others enjoy worshipping in a more outgoing way using song, dance and drama to create a more modern approach to the praise of God.

My first pastorate was on a new housing estate. It was a small, dual purpose building and there were plans to erect a new church because so many young families lived in the area and our building could not accommodate the numbers who were wanting to attend. We had to raise a lot of money for this massive project but the need for extra premises was so immediate that it was decided that a priority was to build some kind of Youth Hall as a temporary measure. Our youth work was growing at such a fast rate that it was imperative to have another building solely for the use of this age group.

An advertisement for some old army huts was spotted in the local paper and from the description and measurements given, they were deemed to be ideal for our purpose. We had several strong and willing young men in the church and they felt sure that they could erect the sections without too much difficulty. The hut was duly ordered. After a time the sections were delivered. The method of construction was that each of the side panels was put up and then these were locked in position by a roof section. The whole structure was not really stable until the second end was erected and all the sections locked and bolted together.
Work started early the following Saturday morning but progress was not as fast as had been hoped and the hut was only half completed as dusk fell. The half-erected building was not as stable as we would have wished so guy ropes were attached to keep the sections in place.

That night a gale blew and as I lay in bed I knew it spelt disaster for our newly erected hut. As soon as it was light on the Sunday morning I cycled to the church and, as I feared, all the sections were flat on the ground. My service for the day had already been prepared, but no one would believe me when I announced the text from Isaiah 54:2,
'Lengthen the ropes and strengthen the stakes.'
I had a ready made introductory illustration!

I'll huff and I'll puff and I'll blow your hut down!

The hall was eventually completed and furnished apart from one item – we needed a piano. It was suggested that there must be some unwanted pianos around and that someone would be kind enough to donate one to the youth club. The Church Secretary was delegated to place an advertisement in 'The Morning News', a local paper which was published daily. There was very little editorial material in this paper, but it was full of adverts so was the ideal place for our request for a piano.

The Church Secretary went ahead with this plan but failed to tell me when the advert was to appear and, more importantly, that he was putting my name as the point of contact. The first thing I knew was when my telephone rang at 7.00am one morning and a lady offered me her piano if we could arrange collection. This phone call was quickly followed by a second and a third of similar ilk. By 8.00am I had received five offers! At the end of the day the number had grown to thirty two pianos! Two people were sent to view all the offers and finally it was decided to accept two instruments and send our grateful thanks to all the other would-be donors.

One of the church members had a trailer and so he, with some assistants, was assigned the task of collecting the two pianos. One of the accepted offers came from a village pub a few miles away. I can only guess what happened when the group arrived at the pub but I know the collection took far longer than was estimated. Eventually they arrived back at the church with two men in the trailer playing the piano and singing at the top of their voices as if rehearsing for a local carnival!

Money was raised from various sources and the time came for work to start on the new church building which was to be erected adjacent to the dual purpose hall. The architect, engineers and foreman oversaw the work as mechanical diggers and workmen began excavating the foundations. When this stage was completed cement mixers and bricks started to arrive. On one particular day, lorry drivers were revving their engines, stacks of bricks were being unloaded, workmen were shouting instructions to one another and amidst all this mayhem I was preparing to conduct a funeral service within the next thirty minutes. I went out and explained the situation to the site foreman and the driver of one of the lorries and stressed that I did not want a lot of noise whilst the service, which would last about thirty minutes, was taking place. The two men looked at their watches and obviously decided the bricks had to be unloaded in record time. They shouted more instructions and every man on site immediately left what they were doing to help with the unloading of the lorry. I have never seen a load of bricks transferred from one place to another so quickly. The whole load was unloaded and the last brick was being stacked just as the hearse arrived at the church door. The men got into their cab and drove off. A tea break was called for the rest of the workers just as I led the pall bearers carrying the coffin into the church. Never has so much been done by so few in such a short space of time.

The church was eventually completed and everyone was delighted with the new place of worship. It was spacious, light and airy. As is normal in a non-conformist church, the walls were plain and a simple empty cross hung in front of a royal blue full length drape at the front of the church. The simplicity and peacefulness of the building helped people focus on the presence of God. Through the plain glass windows the congregation could see the trees and grass of the adjacent playing field but one particularly large window caused problems in the summer. On bright sunny days the sun shone through this window and directly into my face just as I was coming to the end of my sermon. One deacon commented,
"When the sun shines in your eyes it is time to stop."
I then realised that as the season progresses, and the sun gets lower in the sky, my sermons would need to get shorter and shorter if I took his advice.

Sermons

I am passionate about Fairtrade and Traidcraft and I feel very strongly that people in under-developed countries should be able to earn a fair wage for their labours. So often they are exploited and work in dreadful conditions for a meagre wage. The huge profits from their labours are grasped by the already rich countries of the world. Millions of people live in appalling conditions where water is polluted, disease is rampant and famine causes the deaths of many. I enthusiastically promote Fairtrade and Traidcraft whenever I can and encourage church members to purchase goods bearing the Fairtrade logo in order to support the people in the developing world. Fairtrade products are now readily available in all big supermarkets.

One Sunday I was leading a Church service and the focus of my sermon was the need for Christians to support Fairtrade and particularly to buy Fairtrade coffee. I knew that this particular Church served coffee after the service to give the opportunity for people to meet in fellowship together. Furthermore, I knew that the coffee they served was not Fairtrade. When the service was over I imagined that there would be panic in the kitchen because of the views I had expressed. I felt sure that after I had promoted the ethos of fair trade, the consciences of the ladies in the kitchen would not allow them to use another well-known brand which discriminates against the poorest and weakest producers. I wondered what they would do. After the service, I went to collect my cup of coffee.

Surprise, surprise! There was no sign of a coffee jar of any sort. They had tipped their usual brand of coffee out of its familiar jar and into a glass dish to save their embarrassment. The point of the sermon had been made!

It's nice to know that people listen!

Family Services

Over the years many parents have felt embarrassed by the behaviour of their young children in church and so have stopped attending. The services were of little interest to the children and the temptation to run about or make a noise when everything was quiet was a natural reaction. Nowadays many churches are family friendly and arrange some services specifically with children in mind. There are action songs which are catchy and easily learned, there are activities which the children enjoy and there are opportunities for youngsters to learn about God in a happy and lively atmosphere. Some churches are now advertising Tots' Services which last no more than thirty minutes and which are extremely popular.

In the early days of my ministry it was our practice to hold a Family Service every month and to encourage all our uniformed organisations to attend. Many parents who did not normally attend church would come along on these occasions. On one particular Sunday the mother of one of the Beaver Scouts came accompanied by her younger child – a boy of about 3 or 4 years of age. It was quite obvious, from what happened later, that the child had asked the question,
"Why are we going to Church?"
It was also clear that the mother had replied,
"We are going to meet God."

The child and his mother were sitting two rows from the front and the child was standing on the chair looking around the Church. He wasn't going to miss anything because he had been brought to Church to meet God. At the beginning of the service, the vestry door opened and I walked into the Church wearing my clerical gown and stole. The little boy pointed to me and in his highly-pitched voice which was heard by everyone in the church, said, "Is that God?"

One of my talks for family services involves taking a small model of a beehive to Church. During the course of the service I open the hive and take out a cardboard bee. All the bees have names based on Biblical texts. As I introduce each bee to the congregation I ask the bee to whisper in my ear to tell me his name. One is called 'Strong', (Bee Strong); then comes 'Courageous' (Bee Courageous). A story follows the appearance of each bee explaining why we have to adopt these virtues to follow Jesus. At one service everything was going according to plan. When I came to the fifth bee I put the cardboard cut out to my ear for the bee to tell me his name. Nothing was forthcoming. I looked at the bee and explained that all the boys and girls wanted to know his name. I put the cut out to my ear again, but still there was no response from the bee. I looked at the bee in disgust and said, without realising the implication,
"I suppose you are Bee Awkward."
Some of the congregation smiled, but the faces of others showed a look of disgust. The moral is never to ad-lib.

So you're B…. Awkward!

Most churches try to make their premises welcoming but one often wonders what impression the church building has on newcomers and on children who have not been to church before. The building is often big and imposing. The ceilings are high and the pews must seem a very peculiar form of seating to a small child.

A four year old child was in church for the first time. He was intrigued by the enormous organ pipes at the front of the church and he sat still looking at them all through the service. The reason for this fascination became clear when I walked down the aisle after the service. He stepped out in front of me, pointed to the organ pipes, and said,
"When are you going to let all those rockets off?"

Christmas Day is traditionally an occasion when all the family attend church. The turkey is cooking in the oven, presents have been opened by the children, and exhausted parents, who have been awoken by their excited children at an early hour are ready for a short period of calm. As minister, the Christmas morning service was my opportunity to play with the toys which the children had brought along to show during part of the service. The service went just as I had envisaged and as people left afterwards I shook hands with them all and wished them a Happy Christmas. As one family left their little boy, who was about five years of age, came up to me and said,
"Do you know what we are having for dinner?"
I was fairly certain the answer would be 'a turkey', but I wanted him to have the punch line so I replied,
"I just cannot guess, you tell me."

His reply brought laughter to all standing around,
"We're having a dead hen."

Mothering Sunday is another important day which families enjoy. Songs are sung and prayers said thanking God for His love and for all the love a mother gives to her children. It is usual in these services for daffodils or small bunches of spring flowers to be given to each child to present to their Mum. During one Mothering Sunday service held at an Anglican Church the children were given daffodils to take home for their mums. Unfortunately someone had miscalculated and there were not enough flowers for all the children. The vicar knew how disappointed the children would be if they were not able to have any flowers. He went over to the choirboys who had not been given their flowers and whispered to them,
"We haven't enough daffodils left but you can pick some from the graveyard as you go home."

Baptisms

Ministers are often requested to officiate at special services for families. Sometimes it is the joyous occasion of a baptism when relations get together to celebrate the happy event.

My first pastorate was on a new housing estate where there were lots of young married couples. After a year or two of marriage their thoughts turned to raising a family and the midwives and local hospital were kept busy delivering the babies. I paid special visits to the new mothers and dutifully admired their offspring.

New parents often requested that I should baptise their babies. The age group of the local community was such that there was often at least one baptism every month. Incidentally, I did not conduct a funeral service until I had been in that pastorate for three years. At that time the area had the highest birth rate in the West Midlands and I had to be very careful how I reported this. On one occasion I said,
"Since I came to this area it now has the highest birth rate in the West Midlands".
Realising what I had said I hastily had to add,
"I assure you that the high statistics were nothing to do with me!"

They look just like their father!

I had an interesting experience with one baptism. A lady stopped me in the street and asked if she could have her children 'done'. 'Done' was the usual expression used by non-churchgoers when referring to infant baptism. I arranged to call at the lady's home as I wanted to explain what baptism meant and the implications of the promises she and her husband would be asked to make at the service. It is often the case nowadays that people who do not attend church regularly, and feel that they cannot honestly make and keep these promises, are offered an alternative service of Infant Dedication. The full meaning of the two services is carefully explained to the parents.

I arrived at the house on the pre-arranged date to discuss the arrangements for the baptismal service with the parents. I knocked on the door, was invited in and was offered a seat. The mother sat to my left whilst the father was on my right. Father had no interest at all in the discussion and I felt he was there under sufferance. It transpired that not only did they want their baby baptised but also the rest of their large family too. The children ranged in ages from the newly-born baby to the eldest child who was 9 years old. After a lengthy discussion I eventually reached the point where I needed the names of the children and their dates of birth. The mother started with the eldest child and worked down through the family in descending order of age. As she reeled off the names and year in which they were born I wrote the list in my notebook:

First child   1957
Second child 1958
Third child   1959

Then there was a year's gap as the next child had been born in 1961.
At that point father came to life and he sat bolt upright in his chair and shouted out, "What happened in 1960?"
"Oh", said mother, "Our Sally was born in 1960 but we had her done in hospital".

Arrangements then had to be made for the service and it was decided that I would baptise the baby first followed by the other children in age order. The appointed Sunday came and at the appropriate point all the children were lined up in age order as we had arranged.

I had baptised the third child when the eldest girl (the nine year old), realised what was happening and decided to take flight. She raced down the aisle towards the door. Father saw her disappearing and set off in hot pursuit. A few seconds later the two of them reappeared and came back down the aisle. Father wasn't going to let her escape for a second time and kept tight hold of her arm until her turn came. Very reluctantly, she came forward for baptism but wouldn't look up at me and so the water was sprinkled on the top of her head!

The church calendar, the particular circumstances of the family requesting a baptismal service for their child, and also my own family commitments meant that on one occasion we had to take the unusual step of arranging a Baptism and Communion in the same morning service. In some churches those wishing to take communion leave their seats and kneel at the rail at the front of the church to receive the sacraments. However, in the United Reformed Church, the wine and bread for Holy Communion is given in small individual cups which are taken by the Elders to the seated congregation. Also there is what is known as, an 'open' communion table. This means that everyone in the congregation who loves our Lord Jesus Christ is invited to participate in the Lord's Supper, whether or not they are church members.

Now the friends and relations in this particular baptismal party were not regular churchgoers and obviously did not understand the symbolism or procedure. When the Elder went along the row with the tray of individual cups filled with communion wine, one of the party, who was more comfortable in a pub than in a church, took a glass, lifted it up and said,
 "Cheers."

Weddings

The occasion of a marriage is usually a joyous time for the couple, for their families and friends and for all those present. It is the uniting of two people in matrimony with the hope that they will enjoy long and happy lives together. Services held in church have special significance for the couple are making their vows in God's presence.

Sometimes weddings have their amusing moments.
A West Indian couple came to see me to discuss their forthcoming marriage ceremony. They were a lovely couple and they told me they had invited many of their West Indian friends to the wedding. I explained that there are certain parts in the service which I must complete by law, but apart from that, I would willingly model the service on a traditional West Indian wedding if they so wished. I immediately regretted my offer when the bride said,
"At home [meaning Trinidad], we usually have twelve hymns."
I imagined the service lasting for the whole afternoon after which I would have to pacify a very overworked organist. Much to my relief, she then added,
"As we are in England we would like an English service."
I learned my lesson and have never made a similar offer since!

Tradition has it that the bride arrives at the church a little late but on one occasion time ticked away and she was twenty minutes late. At last she arrived at the church door and suddenly realised that she had left her bouquet of flowers at home. I suggested that we should send someone to retrieve the flowers and that the service would start immediately.

I felt sure that the flowers would be there for her to hold after the service when the photographs were taken and that scarcely anyone would notice. However past experience taught me that you never argue with a bride on her wedding day. This bride had decided that she wanted the flowers there and then, and so immediately turned round and uttering the words,
"I'll be back",
got into the bridal car again to go home and get her flowers.

Many brides arrive at church with lovely dresses which often have long trains billowing behind. The yards of material in the train often make it difficult for the bride to get in and out of her car.

I recall one bride wearing a dress with a very, very large bow at the top of the train. As she got out of the car the bow caught on the handle of the car door and became separated from the dress. Panic stations set in. The bride refused to walk down the aisle in her dress minus its bow. There was only one thing we could do to resolve the situation and that was for me to go to the front of the church and make an announcement asking if any lady in the congregation had a needle and thread in her handbag. Fortunately one lady produced the necessary sewing materials and the bride's mother hastily re-attached the bow. We were then able to proceed with the service.

Perhaps the most amusing incident - though it was not funny at the time - was the occasion when the best man brought the ring to church in a little box supplied by the jeweller. At the appropriate moment I went to the best man with the open book on which he was to place the ring. He retrieved the box from his pocket and frantically tried to open it. He was wearing white gloves which hindered his efforts. I whispered,
"Take your gloves off."
Believe it or not, he could not undo the studs on his gloves! He then turned to the bridegroom who managed to undo the stud but the operation of trying to open the box continued. It just would not open. Both bridegroom and best man were getting very embarrassed. The bridegroom snatched the box from his friend's hands but he, too, was unable to open it. In sheer desperation the best man grabbed the box back, put it on the floor and stamped on it. To everyone's relief the box opened! Since then I have always instructed the best man not to have the ring in a box.

There are a lot of details that a Minister needs to ascertain before a wedding takes place. There is a legal obligation to enter these details in the Marriage Register and on the Marriage Certificate. Every three months the Minister or Authorised Person for the church has to submit a copy of the Marriage Register to the local Registrar. Those requesting marriage are asked for their full names, their ages, where they live, their occupations, their fathers' names and details of their marital status.

When one couple came to see me to arrange their wedding I was going through all these details and discovered that the groom was an insurance broker and the bride was his secretary. In the ensuing conversation it transpired that they had invited a large number of people who were their business associates in the world of insurance, to attend the wedding.

We discussed the service and the solemn vows they would take. A few weeks later the wedding ceremony duly took place without any hitches. After the service the happy couple walked down the aisle together followed by the bridal party and all the guests. They assembled outside for the usual photographs. I stayed behind to complete the registers and the marriage certificate. When all the paper work was completed I took the marriage certificate to the happy couple and presented it to the bride. At that moment it began raining and the guests took out their umbrellas. Before my eyes was the biggest selection of advertising umbrellas I had ever seen. There was Norwich Union, Prudential, Standard Life, and many, many more.

Did you insure against rain?

Funerals

Christians believe that the life, death and resurrection of Jesus Christ gives us all the promise of eternal life. A funeral service, or a Thanksgiving Service, as it is often called, is a means of giving thanks to God for the life of a recently deceased person and of committing the deceased to God's love and care.

Taking funeral services is an important part of a minister's work and he or she will make two or three visits to the deceased person's family prior to the actual funeral service and afterwards too. The minister offers comfort and support to the family and discusses the funeral service with them so that the service is a personal and appropriate tribute to the departed. Often families who are in a state of numbness following the death of a loved one, need practical advice about registering the death, finding an undertaker, informing others of the death and planning the funeral service.

If a person is to be cremated it is essential that the funeral director liaises with the crematorium to book a suitable time for the service.

One undertaker contacted me a few days prior to Christmas to ask me to conduct a service at the crematorium. He said the family had really wanted the service before Christmas, but unfortunately the crematorium was fully booked and the earliest available date was December 29th.

I immediately went to visit the family and they told me the same story – they had wanted the service before Christmas but it wasn't possible so they had had to agree that the funeral would take place on the 29th.

Later that same afternoon I had another phone call from the undertaker.
"About that funeral you have agreed to take on the 29th", he said. "Well, we find we can fit it in before Christmas after all. There's been a cancellation at the crematorium for a service on the morning of Christmas Eve."

Now I believe in the resurrection, but this seemed quite ridiculous. I couldn't imagine how a crematorium could have a cancellation. I wondered if there had been a rising from the dead! It transpired that there was a large contingent of relatives from Canada coming to the funeral that had been planned prior to Christmas. Because it was a busy time of year all the flights were fully booked and these relatives had been unable to arrange a flight. Consequently the family had decided to delay the funeral until the Canadian relatives could get to England.

This delay meant that 'my' family could have the date they had originally wanted before Christmas after all.

Not everyone wants a cremation and some families prefer to have their deceased relatives buried in family graves in a cemetery. Preparing a grave is not a straightforward job for the grave diggers. I lived in an area where, during the winter months, the water table was very high. Quite often I would arrive at the graveside to see that bark chippings had been placed in the bottom of the newly dug grave to hide the rising water. I was conducting one burial service just after there had been a bad spell of heavy rain and the water table was very high. As I processed through the cemetery to the spot where the coffin was to be buried I could see the grave digger still in the hole bailing out water as fast as he could. He left it to the very last minute before jumping out and scattering the customary bark chippings on to the water. He approached me as I drew near and said, "For God's sake, Vicar, keep it short. The water is rising too fast".

Despite a minister ensuring that he has visited the family, discussed the deceased person's life with them, planned the service meticulously, and spoken with the funeral director the unexpected can still happen.

On one occasion I conducted a funeral service in church. Everything went according to plan and afterwards the funeral group went to the churchyard for the burial service. We went in a dignified manner and processed between the tombstones to where the coffin was to be buried. I was horrified to discover that the grave had not been dug!

Many people nowadays reach their three score years and ten, and more and more people are still living active lives when they are in the nineties. Because of better diets and improved medical care the number of centenarians is growing rapidly. It is therefore extremely sad when a minister is asked to perform a funeral service for a child or young person. The death of a child can be particularly painful for families who feel that they have lost a dear one whose life has scarcely begun. It is often difficult for them to come to terms with such a loss and it often takes much counselling for relatives to come to terms with these events.

There was a sad occasion when I was asked to conduct a funeral of a young lady. She had been a single mother and was in her mid-thirties. Her young son had died a few years previously and she had retained his ashes. She had been aware that a serious illness would inevitably lead to her own premature death. Accordingly, she had made plans that when she died her son's ashes would be interred with hers. Consequently the boy's grandparents retained his ashes prior to the double internment.

I went to the house to meet the girl's parents who had the sad task of making the arrangements for their daughter's funeral. They explained the situation regarding their grandson's ashes and the plans their daughter had made. I enquired the whereabouts of the boy's ashes.
"Oh", the mother said, "they are on the top of that dresser."
She pointed to the piece of furniture and suddenly the cry went up,
"Where's Justin's ashes?"

The ashes were not in their appointed place. Pandemonium set in as the family chased around the house searching for the urn containing Justin's ashes. The sadness of their bereavement was manifested by the loss of their grandson's urn. Clearly this was not the right atmosphere for a discussion about the arrangements for a funeral. I left with the promise that I would return the next day. Fortunately on my subsequent visit the ashes had been found.

The local crematorium is in a beautiful setting in the midst of a wood. It is a peaceful and tranquil haven away from the sound of traffic and other noise. The closeness of nature in that woodland setting gives great comfort to those who mourn.

When a local farmer died his family held a service at the crematorium to commemorate his life. On returning home after the cremation they decided that it would be rather nice if they took half a dozen of his chickens and a cockerel and released them in the grounds of the crematorium where the farmer's ashes were to be scattered. This they did, but unfortunately, the chickens did not last long because the local fox ensured that he had a good supper. The cockerel, however, eluded the fox for some time and the crematorium staff became attached to him. The men who drove the hearses and the funeral cars to the crematorium would feed the cockerel with scraps of food whilst the service was in progress. The cockerel became quite tame and when he saw the funeral cars approaching, would fly up on to the canopy at the entrance to the chapel to await the titbits of food.

No one minded this unusual visitor until one day, when I was taking a service, I had just pressed the button for the curtain to close around the coffin when the cockerel crowed.

For whom the cock crows

Visiting

Ministers spend a lot of time visiting people in their homes and, by doing this, get an insight into the home lives of the community. Some homes are very attractive and well cared for whilst others can be drab, somewhat dirty and unattractive.

I went to one home which fell into the latter category and, soon after my arrival I was offered a cup of tea. I found an excuse not to accept this hospitality. The same thing happened the next time I went to visit. On the third occasion I felt I could not refuse the offer of a cup of tea yet again. The lady went into the kitchen and returned shortly afterwards carrying a tray on which were two cups and saucers. I looked at them and realised I had to drink from one of these cups, neither of which looked particularly clean. She handed a cup and saucer to me and I decided to turn the cup round and drink using my left hand. By doing this, I thought, the side that touched my lips was possibly the lesser used side and therefore the cleaner. She spotted what I had done and said,
"Oh, Mr Carrier, are you left handed too?"

I'm not really ambidextrous!

Church Notice Boards

I did not preach in my own church every single Sunday of the year. Sometimes there were 'exchange Sundays' when all the ministers in the area would preach in one of the other local churches. The idea was to give both clergy and congregations a change of scenery. There were also Sundays when Lay Preachers led the services in my church and this enabled me to preach elsewhere. Small village churches, where there was no regular incumbent, especially welcomed an ordained minister to conduct the service of Holy Communion and so occasionally I would lead a service in one of these churches.

I visited one church where there was the custom of putting the name of the preachers on the outside notice board behind a glass screen.
It said:
  'This Sunday:………………..'
and below:
  'Next Sunday:………………..'

I arrived at the Church accompanied by one of my daughters. She saw the notice board and said,

"Dad, you've got some opposition next week."
I looked at the notice board and it said,
  'This Sunday: The Rev. John Carrier.'
  'Next Sunday: The Messiah'

That looks like a case of mistaken identity!

Special Services

Sometimes I have been invited to conduct a special service, perhaps a Church Anniversary or a Harvest Service, as a special guest preacher. This is quite an honour and usually there is a large congregation for these special occasions. Often the service differs from the usual sandwich of hymns, prayers and readings, and special anthems are sung or greetings read out from people unable to be present. At these times the church has a printed Order of Service so that the congregation is aware of the pattern the service will take.

After one of these special services there was opportunity for the congregation to greet one another in the adjoining hall and to renew friendships with people who had travelled a distance whilst enjoying a cup of tea, coffee and refreshments. Whilst I was having my drink a very attractive young lady came up to me with the printed Order of Service and asked if she could have my autograph. Now it makes an old man feel really great when an attractive young lady wants his autograph. I duly obliged and felt chuffed. As I handed it back to her I joked,
"There you are, you can treasure that".
"Oh", she replied, "its not for me, it's for my grandma".

Some years ago I was invited to conduct an Advent service at a village church. The church was decorated for Christmas with a majestic Christmas tree, a nativity scene, beautiful floral arrangements and various seasonal displays around the church. It all looked absolutely lovely and people had spent a lot of time and effort to make the church look so attractive.
However, there was one problem. When the organist started to play the electric organ the Christmas lights on the tree went out. Obviously there was some problem with the electrics. A couple of men in the congregation went forward to attempt to fix it, but they had no success. The service began. I announced the first hymn. The organist started playing and as we stood to sing, out went the lights on the tree. At that point a lady in the congregation walked to the front clasping her handbag. This lady lives on a long boat on the canal which runs through the village. She carries out all her own boat repairs and is a very practical person. She opened her handbag – not to get out her make-up, but to retrieve screwdrivers and pliers from her mobile tool kit. She promptly realised what the problem was and, to everyone's delight, fixed the faulty wiring before putting the tools back into her handbag. The task was completed just as the hymn ended and as she walked past me back to her seat, she said in a voice which I am sure everyone in the church heard,
"The men don't like it when I fix things that they can't".

Chaplaincy

Each hospital has chaplains who offer spiritual care to patients, relatives and staff. Being a Chaplain is an important role for it gives the opportunity of touching people's lives at times when they can be experiencing great crises or pain. Frequently within the hospital environment there are those who feel frightened and alone and those who are suffering or approaching death. The Chaplain is the person to whom they turn, who can be an understanding friend and confidant and who can listen to people and respond sensitively by offering spiritual care.

For several years I was a chaplain at Warwick Hospital and on one occasion I went in to visit a Free Church patient. On his admission form he had indicated that he was a Methodist and so he was on my 'Free Church' list. I discovered that he was a homeless man, who travelled from place to place on foot and I learnt a great deal about his itinerant lifestyle from my conversations with him. He was in hospital for several weeks and I got to know him quite well. One day he said to me,
"Padre, will you bring me a small bottle of whisky?"
I told him I could not do that, and, even if I were willing to do so, the nurses would confiscate it as soon as they saw it on his locker.
He replied,
"Oh, I wouldn't put it on the locker, I would put it under there."
He pointed under the sheets.

"You couldn't do that", I replied, "as soon as they make the bed they will find it".

"Oh no they won't", he retorted.

At that point his leg appeared from under the bedclothes and I saw that he was wearing socks. He explained that he had told the nurses he had cold feet, but that the real reason for his wearing socks was so that he would be able to hide the bottle of whisky down the sock when I took it to him.

He remained a disappointed man for I never took him his whisky. As I have since said,

"He is the only person in all my ministry who I have knowingly refused to help spiritually."

Quite often when I visited a patient there would be flowers on the locker. (This was in the era before hospitals had realised that flowers in vases of water were harbingers of germs.)

On one occasion there was a pot plant standing on a lady's locker. When it was brought in by a relative it must have looked really beautiful but when I saw it, it was obviously suffering through lack of water. A water jug was on the lady's locker and so I used it to give the plant a good long drink and hoped it would revive. A few minutes later a nurse came down the ward. She looked at the nearly empty jug of water and said,

"Ah, Mrs Jones, I see you're drinking a lot of water. That's good. Now let me measure how much is left in the jug and then I'll know how much you have drunk."

I must confess that I didn't own up, but I did have a good laugh with the patient once the nurse had disappeared.

Another part of my chaplaincy duties was to visit the patients in a mental hospital. Most of the wards were locked as many of the patients would have wandered off. Some of the patients had lived there for many years. There were several very lonely people whose families rarely visited them and they had become extremely institutionalised.

I spent one afternoon each week visiting the patients at the hospital. I would sit and chat to them and we would go over the same topics week in and week out. One week one of the ladies said,
"We like you coming to see us, we feel you're one of us."

Apocrypha

From time to time the clergymen of different denominations in a town meet together, in what used to be called 'Ministers' Fraternals' The aim of the meetings is to pray together and to plan ways in which the different churches can work together cooperatively. The name may well have changed now as there are so many female clergy and the word 'Fraternal' is not really appropriate.

Churches of different denominations are not in competition with each other but all have the one aim, to serve God and to bring the Christian message of love and tolerance to those in the community.

As well as attending the Fraternals I often had separate meetings with the local Anglican vicar. Our churches were on the same estate and we worked in close cooperation. On one occasion he invited me to visit him and when I arrived at the vicarage he showed me into his study. On the wall I noticed a huge map of the area and coloured pins had been inserted on several roads. I looked at the map closely and enquired if the pins signified the houses of his parishioners. I wondered if the different colours indicated which church activities the people living in that house attended. Perhaps the blue pins were for members of the Mothers' Union; red pins indicated members of the PCC and green pins showed the homes of choir members.

He roared with laughter.
"Oh", he said, "It's nothing like that. I study that map before I go visiting so that I don't mix my drinks!"

Teeth can be a problem for public speakers.
I had visited the dentist one Thursday before my preaching engagement on the following Sunday. I was having a crown attached to my front tooth. I didn't envisage any problem as there were two clear days to get used to it before I had to preach. I felt sure all would be well. What I did not anticipate was a fitting problem. The dentist could not complete the treatment and so a temporary crown was used but he assured me that this would not cause any problems when I was preaching. Two days later as I led the service, everything was going well until part way through the sermon. The new crown suddenly dropped out and fell onto the pulpit floor. I immediately realised what had happened. I could feel the gap in the front of my mouth, but there was nothing for it but to ignore what had happened and carry on. In the hymn following the sermon I bent down and retrieved the crown and put it in my pocket.

After the service 'Gappy' was shaking hands with the members of the congregation as they left. One brave soul asked me, "What happened during the sermon? I saw something white fly across your gown and disappear behind the pulpit. Did you see it?"
"No madam", I replied. "I didn't see it, I only felt it! Strange things can happen in churches!"
I didn't tell her the true reason for the white flying object!

There goes another pearl of wisdom!

When one travels through towns and villages there is often a sign announcing the name of the place and underneath it says, 'Twinned with ……..' and gives the name of a continental town. Links are made between the two locations and often reciprocal visits are made. The idea is to foster good international relationships.

Synods, groups of churches and occasionally individual churches endeavour to foster similar links.

A church where I was Interim Moderator had a close tie with a German Church on the Palatinate in Germany. Exchange visits were arranged between members of the two communities and these were greatly enjoyed by everyone. I was at that church on one occasion when the German party visited. Generally speaking, their language skills were very good, but occasionally a word occurred during the conversation which meant they had to look in their dictionaries for a translation. On this particular evening a group of us were sitting together when one of the Germans asked a rather prim and proper English lady what she did for a living. She replied that she was a solicitor's clerk. A puzzled expression appeared on the faces of the Germans and they took out their dictionaries. Suddenly their puzzled expressions turned to shock and we couldn't understand the reason for this. We looked at the translation in their dictionaries and suddenly realised why there was such consternation. They had looked up the word 'Soliciting'!

When I go to the supermarket with Marjorie to do the shopping we may pass a lady whom I know and I greet her. As soon as we are out of ear-shot, Marjorie is quick to ask,
"Who was that?"
I tell her that it was a girl I married.
Marjorie, who for many years was a teacher, retaliates when she stops to speak to a man who I do not recognise. It is then my turn to ask,
"Who was that?"
Marjorie replies, "That's the father of one of my children".

Churches are frequently involved with raising money for local charities, supporting good causes, helping those in need, giving to the underprivileged and raising awareness about issues which treat certain sections of the community unfairly.

Ministers, together with their congregations, often provide a pivotal and practical role in this sort of work. One group with which I was involved was planning to take a party of young people with disabilities who were mostly in wheelchairs, on a trip to London. Each member of the party needed an able-bodied carer to accompany them and so I volunteered. Many of the youngsters had never been to London before and it was a great adventure for them. When we arrived in the capital we were given an itinerary and toured the usual sights. I pushed a lad in a wheelchair and we marvelled at the important buildings we saw together. We visited Buckingham Palace, Trafalgar Square, Big Ben, The Houses of Parliament etc. We came up Whitehall to

Horse Guards Parade and saw a mounted guardsman by his sentry box. 'My' lad wanted to be photographed at the side of the mounted guardsman and asked me to take the picture. It was a hot day and he posed for the photo as he sat in his wheelchair holding a can of coke in one hand. I was about to take the picture when a tourist walked in front of me and pushed 20p into this lad's coke can thinking he was collecting for charity!

I feel that it is very important that Christian people should not be solely active in groups connected to the church but should meet with non-churchgoers too. In this way others realise that Christians are not a breed apart but that they have their good points and their difficulties just like everyone else.

I am involved in several secular groups and sometimes when I am in the company of people who do not go to church and things aren't going very well they will let out the occasional swear word to relieve their emotions. Immediately they realise what they have just said and turn to me to apologise. One man was ranting to me about a certain incident which had occurred and about which he certainly was not pleased. His tirade was punctuated with some choice swear words. Suddenly he realised what he had said and that he was speaking to me, 'a man of the cloth'. He began the usual "Sorry, Vicar…." and then quickly added, "But I needn't apologise to you now, it doesn't count, because you're retired."

AMEN